Creative Fashion Illustration

How to Develop Your Own Style

Creative Fashion Illustration

Stuart McKenzie

BLOOMSBURY

LONDON · NEW DELHI · NEW YORK · SYDNEY

Bloomsbury Visual Arts
An imprint of Bloomsbury Publishing Plc

50 Bedford Square
London
WC1B 3DP
UK

1385 Broadway
New York
NY 10018
USA

www.bloomsbury.com

**Bloomsbury is a registered trade mark of
Bloomsbury Publishing Plc**

British Library Cataloguing-in-Publication Data
A catalogue record for this book is available from the British Library.

ISBN: PB: 9780857858290
HB: 9780857858283

Library of Congress Cataloging-in-Publication Data
McKenzie, Stuart (Illustrator)
Creative fashion illustration : how to develop your own style / Stuart
McKenzie.
pages cm
ISBN 978-0-85785-829-0 (paperback) -- ISBN 978-0-85785-828-3
(hardback) -- ISBN 978-1-4725-8349-9 (electronic) 1. Fashion drawing.
I. Title.
TT509.M39 2014
741.6′72--dc23
2014001621

Internal and cover design by Untitled
Project management by Precision Graphics
Printed and bound in China

Contents

Introduction

From my experience of working in the fashion industry, whether illustrating collections for fashion designer Vivienne Westwood, working for magazines such as U.S. *Cosmopolitan* where I was beauty illustrator, or creating trend-forecasting illustrations for clients such as Marks and Spencer, I have learned that, just as there is no right or wrong way to design a cutting-edge collection, there is no right or wrong way to illustrate fashion. All you need are a set of techniques to experiment with creatively.

Packed full of tips and tricks, this book will help you develop your own style of illustration, not by following prescriptive rules, diagrams, or rigid instructions, but by trying out simple exercises designed to expand your horizons and help you discover your personal strengths as an illustrator. If you are coming to fashion illustration for the very first time, a student looking to develop your technique to gain a more personalized style, or even an experienced illustrator seeking fresh approaches, this book will help build up your core drawing skills and unleash your creativity. The exercises outlined over the following pages continue to be effective in improving my own work. Students I have taught—of all ages and abilities—have found these techniques have helped them to improve as well.

The chapters in the book deal with all the key skills and approaches, explaining their various uses in fashion illustration specifically, starting with simple concepts such as line and later tackling more challenging areas such as fabric renderings and hands and feet. Each chapter builds upon the one before, resulting in a snowball effect of ideas and application of media that can be used together to good effect. I recommend tackling these in chapter order the first time, but after that you can dip in at any section to practice particular skills, shake up old ideas, and use it as a springboard to develop your own methods. If you have one way of drawing, open up to new approaches: For instance we don't always have to start at the head when drawing the figure; we can start with the silhouette, then fill in light and shade, then add details. We can also draw from the inside out, starting with light and shade first, adding detailing, and then the silhouette—a less conventional approach can result in a different feel and often a more interesting illustration.

Through practice and experimentation, drawing on the basic techniques and approaches outlined in this book, you will build up your confidence, develop a unique fashion illustration style, and create lively, exciting work.

I would like to thank the following people for their patience, support, and inspiration in the making of this book: Dahren Davey, Michaela Callaghan, Alexis Panayiotou, Audrey Ang, Lisa Kelly, Gill Stark, and all those who have championed my creativity along the way.

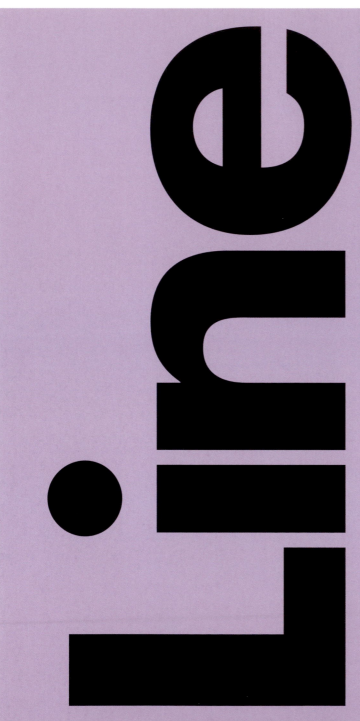

Line is a key element of both fashion and illustration. We can describe fashion in terms of line, for example the lines of a Grecian inspired column dress by Valentino or the twists and turns of a draped dress by Madeleine Vionnet. Working with line, an illustrator can capture the fluidity of the draping or the structure of the pleats. How we represent these qualities in a garment depends on our choice of medium (pen, pencil, paint, etc.) and how we use it to create line—whether thin, thick, fast, or slow.

The exercises in this chapter will get you experimenting with different line styles. I recommend doing each exercise in order and finishing off by reflecting on your work to establish which approaches produce the best results for you. But first, let's begin by warming up.

Warm Up!

When doing any sport or activity, you will perform best if you warm up first; it is no different with drawing/sketching. Warming up will help prepare you effectively for illustration.

- Stand up for this exercise. I think that standing at a desk or an easel is often better when drawing, as it gives you more command over your work.
- Take a soft pencil—anything from a 2b to a 6b because these always give the best soft lines—and hold it at its end between your thumb, index, and forefinger. (Drawings look tight and rigid when a pencil is clutched at its tip.)
- On an 11 x 17 (A3) piece of paper, draw a figure 8 starting at the center. Continue to draw the figure 8 for a few seconds more.
- Eventually, break away from the figure 8 and start to scribble all over the surface of the paper with one continuous line.
- Try not to lift your pencil off the paper while also working your scribbles into the corners; ultimately the whole sheet should be covered.

Continuous Line

Now that we have warmed up, let's experiment with continuous line, a style of drawing that forms the basis of my own illustration practice. This technique involves drawing one continuous line without lifting your pen, pencil, or other medium off the paper. It can be used to achieve a wide variety of results depending on where you start drawing and what medium you use.

Here is an example of a technique I use. Using a picture as a reference and a brush pen as my medium, I've drawn a model's head and shoulders, starting at his nose. I've worked my way around his head, eventually ending up at his shoulders. Note how I've also doubled back, going over the same lines twice.

Exercise 1

Changing Hands, Mediums, and Working "Blind"

For this exercise you'll need an 11 x 17 (A3) piece of paper, a magazine image showing the head and shoulders of a person, and any drawing medium you wish. Follow these instructions, drawing the magazine image with one continuous line and remembering not to pick your medium up off the paper. No cheating!

- Place your paper in landscape orientation (on its side) and divide it into four unequal sections.
- In one of the smallest spaces on your paper, draw the image using one continuous line.
- In the second smallest space, draw with one continuous line using your other hand.
- In the medium-sized space, draw with one continuous line without looking at your paper.

In the next exercise, you will move on to use the largest space on your page to draw a figure from head to toe.

Exercise 2   **Working Quickly**

Find a magazine image of a model showing the full length of the body. It can be a male or female model in a posed, static shot or in motion. Use a different medium from Exercise 1 (if you used a pencil there, you could try a pen or crayon).

For this exercise you'll need to time yourself, so be sure you have some sort of timing device. You'll have 3 seconds to draw each section of the body before moving to the next. Again, do not take your medium off the paper.

- Start at the head.
- Move to the left foot.
- Then move to the left hand.
- Move back up to the neck, then down to the right hand.
- Move down to the right foot.
- Complete the rest of body and elements of clothing.

Your paper will now resemble this.

Note: I haven't always gotten the results I wanted. I call these "tests" or "successful failures." In this example, I drew the head too big and tried alternate mediums. I always keep these tests, as there are qualities in them that can inspire further experimentation.

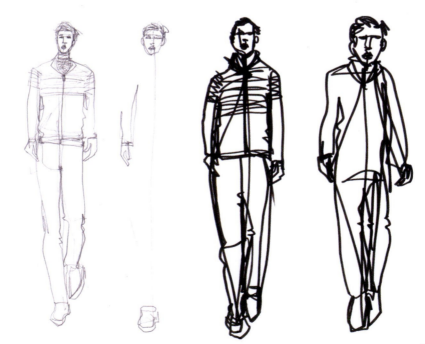

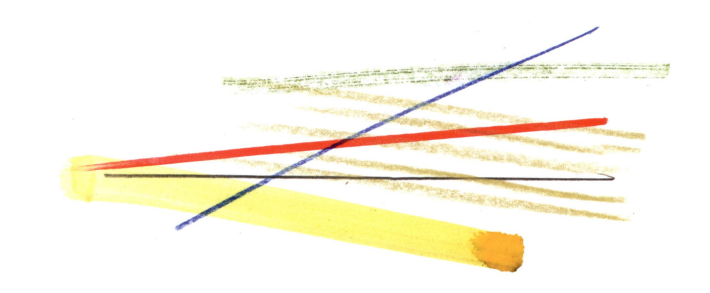

Exercise 3

**Exploring
Different Styles**

You'll need a range of different mediums and an 11 x 17 (A3) piece of paper (or larger) for this exercise. A roll of lining paper (wallpaper liner) can be good—it is inexpensive and you can stick it to a wall to work in a slightly larger format if you wish.

– Make a series of lines using your different mediums.
– Draw while listening to different types of music. Does a change in background music inspire different types of line?

Assess Your Work

By practicing the exercises in this first chapter you have achieved:

- Improved hand-eye coordination
- An ability to sketch quickly to capture what is in front of you. This is an important skill for fashion professionals, when taking visual notes at fashion shows, for example.
- An understanding of different ways to approach line drawing

Notice the different qualities of line in your work and reflect on the techniques and approaches you've used to create them.

- How does the "blind" drawing compare to the others? Does it look looser or more spontaneous?
- What effect did using your other hand have on your drawing?
- How did you work with less time? Did the time limitation produce better results since you had less time to think?
- Which medium did you work better with? Why?

silhouette

In the previous chapter we focused on line. Another way we can look at fashion is shape or, another word more commonly used in fashion, silhouette. Think of the most famous silhouettes from costume and fashion's rich history: the full pleated skirts and dramatic nipped-in waists of Christian Dior's "New Look" of the late 1940s or, to go back even further, the wide pannier-hooped underskirts of the eighteenth century and the crinolines of the nineteenth century. When we illustrate fashion, it's important to bear the silhouette and current mood in fashion in mind as a way of rendering an illustration.

The following exercises will help you develop various ways of representing silhouette and mixing it with the idea of line.

Exercise 1

Silhouettes Using Line

You'll need a few images from a magazine with strong silhouettes; a variety of different media, both wet and dry (pencils, oil pastels, ink, and watercolors, for example); and an 11 x 17 (A3) piece of paper.

- Using one of the magazine images as a model, draw a silhouette, starting at any point and working your way around until you have completed it.

- Draw additional silhouettes using a different medium for each, mixing wet and dry. Make sure you pay attention to the outside line and the nuances, including all the subtle curves and shapes. See how detailed you can be. Allow the silhouettes to overlap and see how they work together to produce an interesting composition.

Exercise 2

Silhouettes Using Shade

For this exercise you will need to work with a new silhouette. Use a pencil for this one, as it works best for scribbling. Instead of drawing with line, try "blocking" it in with scribbles as you go, gradually building up the silhouette.

– Start with a scribbling motion, as if you're doodling.
– Begin to move, fleshing out the figure (I'm fleshing out in a clockwise fashion in the illustration, but you don't have to), paying attention to the shape and all the subtle curves and straight lines.

– Keep scribbling until you have the complete figure.

This is a good exercise to see if you can gauge the size of the figure as you go and make sure you can fit the feet in. Some people's drawings end up being too big and go off the page, while others are too tiny in the center of the page. If either of these issues occurs for you, a bit of practice will improve matters quickly.

Exercise 3

Experimenting with Silhouette and Media

Using different media and scribble techniques will create a range of effects. For this exercise, you can refer to magazine images for silhouette ideas or just make up your own.

– Draw a series of silhouettes in different media using the scribble technique. Get used to the feel of each of the different media and how they respond to what you are doing.
– Vary the poses of the silhouettes, with lively poses mixed with more static poses.

– Notice how you have to tighten up the scribbles to keep the shape and smaller details within the silhouette. Simultaneously work with looser scribbles and tighter scribbles to intensify the shapes more.

Exercise 4   **Stenciling**

Stenciling is an excellent way to develop silhouettes. In this example, I've used stenciling paper to create a silhouette. The paper is quite thick, so you can reuse use the stencil without the edges becoming damaged. You'll need a sharp craft knife to cut your stencil.

–   Try some experimenting in your sketchbook. In one version, I've used inks with a paintbrush, and crayon is used for another. Notice how it accidentally picks up some texture as it's rendered. (We'll look at texture in a later chapter.)

- Gather a series of strong silhouettes from magazines. Choose silhouettes that you feel have something unique and interesting about them.
- Try other ways of working with the stencil. I've used paint, and I've also scribbled though using pencil lines.

**Mixing Line
and Silhouette
Together**

Choose a suitable magazine image to work from. For this exercise, it is important to choose images that show full bodies of models in outfits where the top and bottom parts of clothing are clearly defined. We will be using different media to define different areas of the drawing, so choosing your outfit is important. Catwalk images are ideal for this.

STOP and START, each time picking up a new medium. The color of the medium you choose doesn't have to match the color of the garment.

- START by blocking in the lower section/legs. STOP.
- START from the head; draw the silhouette down to the hand. STOP.
- START by drawing the head, top, and other hand with a continuous line. STOP.

- START blocking in hands and feet. STOP.
- START putting a wash of color on the top/shirt. You create a color wash by adding a lot of water to your paint. STOP.
- START give yourself a minute and add a few more elements, such as a pattern or other wardrobe accessories, like a hat, belt, or scarf. STOP.

How did your finished illustration turn out?
Were there any details you missed that made
it look less convincing? In the example here,
perhaps drawing the negative space separating
the legs would have helped define the trousers
more and made it clearer that the model
is walking.

Sketchbook Practice

Experiment further with silhouette in your sketchbook. Work across a double page and see how the composition works. Try not to be precious and perfectionistic with your approach!

In the example shown on the opposite page, I've worked with three different media: ink, marker pen, and pencil crayon. The silhouette was stenciled first, followed by adding line along the shape of the stencil. Try varying the thickness of the line to add weight to the various sides of the silhouette. Also try getting a balance of half shape and half line to give an interesting effect.

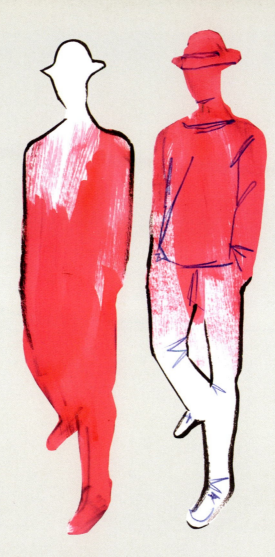

Assess Your Work

In this chapter you experimented with silhouette and combining silhouette with line, including:

- Using line for a basic shape as well as for depicting areas of detail
- Using shape with different media to create varied effects
- Experimenting with scale to fit drawings to a particular page size
- Using stencils to produce silhouettes
- Mixing line and shape, testing the qualities of different media

Consider the effects produced by using these varied approaches to silhouette.

- What impact did the choice of medium have in the exercises?
- Did stopping and starting give your illustration a particular feel?
- How did overlapping your silhouettes change the composition?
- Can a combination of line and shape produce a more complex illustration?

Light & Shade

Creating areas of light and shade will dramatically enhance your work by giving depth to particular areas of interest. Think of famous works of art and imagine the diminished, or at least very different, impact they would have without areas of light and shade. The tonal areas we are looking at in this chapter are those nearest to (lighter) and furthest from (darker) a light source. Figuring out how to effectively use tone in your work will make a considerable difference to your illustration style.

These exercises will help you develop an eye for tone and an ability to play with it to produce multiple effects.

Identifying Light and Shade

Choose an image of a person that has strong tonal contrast and study it for a while. Squint a bit and try and see the figure in terms of the lighter and darker areas. Take two contrasting media, one for the darker shades and one for the lighter; the colors do not need to match. Fill in freehand or trace the lighter and darker areas. To make the process easier, you can use a light box or a piece of paper on a light source, such as a window, for a similar effect.

Focus on the darker and lighter shades and ignore the mid-tones.

- Draw the silhouette.
- Trace or fill in all the darker areas.
- Trace or fill in the lighter areas.

You can choose whether to render the areas of the darker shade or lighter shade first.

If you prefer, you can first trace the light and dark areas separately as shown here, then use your tracings as a guide to fill in those areas with your two chosen media.

Exercise 2

Mixing Light, Shade, Line, and Silhouette

For this exercise, you'll need an image of a full-length figure, which can be either male or female. We are now going to draw the figure combining everything we have learned so far: line, silhouette, light, and shade.

- Draw in the silhouette of the figure.
- Draw in the darker areas.
- Add line detail.

Exercise 3　　**Refresher Exercise**

- Crumple a piece of letter-sized (A4) paper and place it in front of you.
- On a second sheet of letter-sized paper, draw the crumpled paper with one continuous line.
- Draw it again without looking at what you are drawing.

- Draw it again with your alternate hand; this time bring in some light and shade.
- Draw it again, overlapping with your first drawing using a mixture of straight and curved lines.
- Keep this drawing safe, as we will use it in the next chapter.

Assess Your Work

Light and shade can be used in several ways to enhance your fashion illustrations. An understanding of light and shade is essential; from creating subtle tonal differences in your work to dark, dramatic depth, these techniques are essential to master for your portfolio and future professional practice.

By practicing the exercises in this chapter you have learned how to:

- Develop your own distinctive style through the use of light and shade
- Effectively use light and shade to add tone and depth to your work
- Understand how shade can be used to create innovative illustrative effects
- Use light and shade to build on your existing knowledge of line and silhouette

Using light and shade in your drawings will have a dramatic effect. Continue investigating how to use shading to your advantage by considering the following questions:

- Do you find adding areas of shade first easier or harder than adding or outlining areas of light first? Does adding shade or light first change the way your drawings look in any way?
- Do you find it easier to add line detail before or after adding areas or shade?
- Now that you are focusing on light and shade, how has your personal style changed?

Collage (and photomontage) can deliver dynamic and unpredictable results. The work of artists belonging to the Dada, Surrealist, and Pop Art movements, such as Kurt Schwitters, Hannah Höch, and Richard Hamilton, shows how the juxtaposition of images can be used to startling effect.

Materials for collage can be sourced inexpensively and imaginatively from all around you. It's a great way to use up old magazines, newspapers, fabric swatches, theater, cinema, and travel tickets and a good opportunity to try unexpected materials like pressed leaves or flowers. You could even try using traditional methods like making your own glue by mixing flour and water.

In this chapter you will expand your repertoire through working with collage to create lively and imaginative illustrations.

Collage

Exercise 1

Collage Silhouette

Use 11 x 17 (A3) paper, glue, and a magazine for this exercise.

- Tear out as many swatches of color, pattern, and texture from the magazine as you can.
- Create a collage on the piece of paper quickly, without too much thought, and cover the whole surface of the paper, sticking the pieces down with glue.

- When you have finished, turn the paper over and tear out an imagined silhouette of a figure.
- When finished, notice how unpredictably areas of color, texture, and pattern can randomly add to the silhouette giving the impression of clothing.

Exercise 2　　**Model Monster**

This exercise is inspired by the work of the Surrealists. To complete it, you will need a range of materials for your collage and some glue.

- Give yourself 30 minutes to find and cut out as many interesting segments, body parts, objects, patterns, and textures from magazines and newspapers as you can. Use images from a wide variety of sources so you have a good selection of different images to use.

- Play around with scale—use large and small elements—but don't overthink what you are choosing.
- Reassemble all your cut-out images together while being as inventive as you can with your composition.
- Take your Model Monster and do a tonal drawing with a soft pencil (anything from 2–6b). Draw what you see. Did you flinch at the thought of drawing so much detail? We'll look more at drawing design detail in a future chapter, but this is a great start!

For this you'll need an assortment of old magazines and newspapers.

– Tear out a torso shape and stick it roughly in the center of your paper—here I've used an old faded piece of construction paper (which, incidentally, can add an interesting vintage feel to your work)

– Let the torso you have chosen dictate how you will place other body parts and shapes. Play with scale to create a more dynamic effect.
– Tear, rather than cut, your pieces and see how it has a much more spontaneous feel than the previous collage, which was carefully cut. Notice the difference between the two.

Exercise 4   **Mix It Up!**

You'll need a magazine and some scissors for this exercise.

- Choose a full-page image from a magazine featuring an outfit with an interesting silhouette.
- Choose three more full pages from a magazine that have interesting patterns, colors, or textures.
- Layer all four pages with your silhouette image on the top.
- Cut around the silhouette and through the other full-page layers so you end up with four cut out silhouettes, one for each of your chosen pages.

- Cut up each body or silhouette into sections.
- Now mix up the cut shapes and reassemble them into interesting compositions of the figure.
- You can also flip the shapes to reverse them too. Include elements of the original image in the line up. Notice how certain areas are defined by the collage and also give depth to the figures for an edgier feel.

This idea accidentally presented itself to me after I'd left a stencil on top of a pile of paper. I really liked the idea that, by mixing different cut out silhouettes, you can finesse the random nature of the composition to create really striking images.

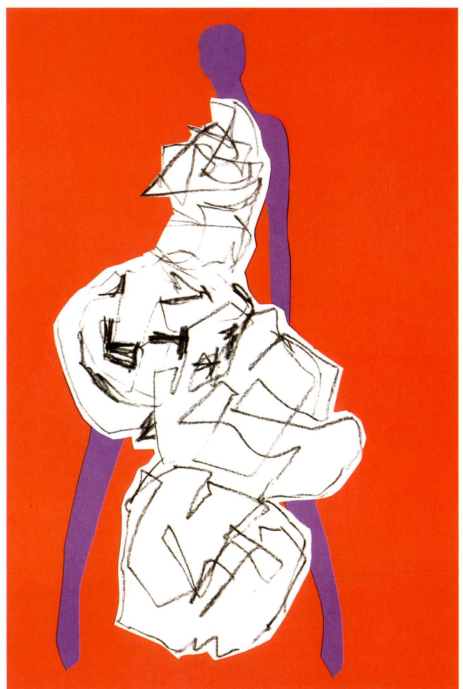

Exercise 5

Instant Couture!

You'll need some heavier drawing paper of assorted colors for this exercise and a silhouette to trace/cut around. If you would like to lengthen your chosen figure, a good tip is to move the silhouette you are tracing around down the page as you trace.

– Take your cut-out silhouette and place it on another sheet of paper of a contrasting color.

– Next take the drawings of the crumpled paper from the Light & Shade chapter, cut around it, and place it on top of your silhouette.
– I've adapted the drawing slightly to make it work with the silhouette, which I've also flipped. See how unpredictably the collaged drawing of the screwed-up paper acts as a garment for an instant couture look!

Assess Your Work

Working with collage gives you the freedom to play with illustration in new and exciting ways.

Upon completing the exercises in this chapter you will have learned:

– To work with mixed media
– To mix line, shape, and collage together
– To enhance your knowledge of silhouette and shape
– That sometimes the best illustrations can be spontaneous accidents. There is no such thing as the right way to illustrate, especially when it comes to fashion!
– To think about composition and how your illustrated figure works on the page

Keep experimenting with collage and review the work you have completed in this chapter by asking yourself the following questions:

– Do you like the collage aesthetic? Why?
– How would you emphasize particular details using collage, for example, buttons or fringing on a dress?
– Does your own personal style of illustration lend itself better to ripped or carefully torn images from magazines when making a collage?
– Are you able to highlight areas of light or shade using collage? How would you do this?

Fashion is as much about fabric as it is about style or form. Understanding the properties of different fabrics, textures, and patterns and being able to depict them within your illustrations, allows you to visually explain to others how a particular garment should look and feel.

It's helpful to practice with different media when trying to convey the characteristics of certain fabrics. Once you have tried out a few, you will develop a feel for which medium works best for the texture you are trying to show. Pay attention to particular types of paper you use too—try different thicknesses and colors of paper, watercolor paper, etc.—and see how they hold paint differently. You could use construction paper (which is inexpensive and comes in a variety of colors) for pastel crayons, special layout papers for marker pens, photocopier paper, or even make your own eco-friendly recycled paper.

These exercises will foster flexible and creative approaches to showing textures, fabrics, and patterns in fashion illustration.

Fabrics, Texture, Pattern

Exercise 1

Mark Making and Pattern

For this exercise you will need an 11 x 17 (A3) sheet of paper and an assortment of wet and dry media.

– Choose a figure from a magazine that has a strong silhouette to use as the basis for a stencil. Cut out the figure, then cut out the head, hands, and feet, and keep these separate.
– Gather as many materials around you as you can (a mixture of wet and dry media) and begin to make marks, patterns, lines, and dots using your stencil on your paper.

– See if you can use improvised implements for making marks, such as sticks, pins, your fingers, or string—anything to give you unpredictable results or splashes of color.
– Try not to wet the edge of the stencil too much (unless you've used special stenciling paper). Be careful not to overwork the mark making. When you you feel you have created enough marks, remove the stencil. Does your figure look like it's enveloped in a wild printed ensemble?

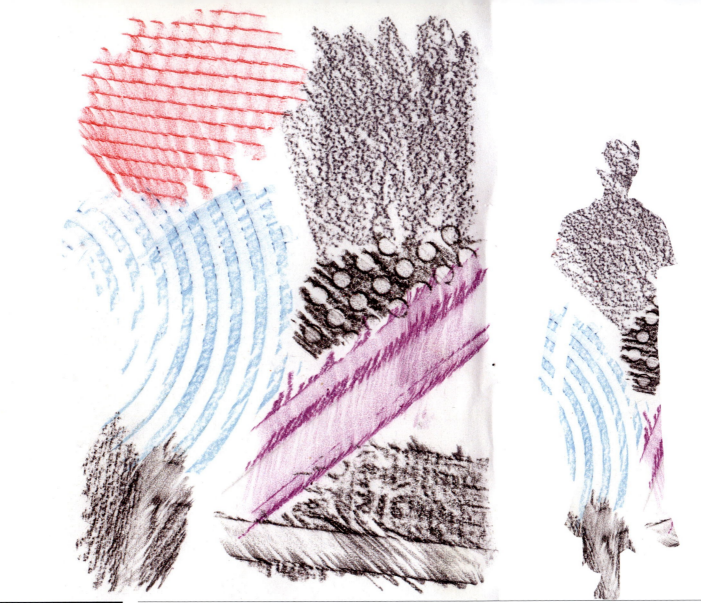

Exercise 2   **Texture**

Take an 11 x 17 (A3) piece of paper (photocopy paper is ideal for this as it is not too thick) and at least three wax crayons of contrasting colors.

- Find as many textures inside or outside as you can and take "rubbings" of these to fill your paper.
- Let the patterns overlap and make them a reasonable size. These will be used for collage, so keep that in mind.

- Using the stencil you created for Exercise 1 as a template, place this onto your textures, draw around it, and cut it out.
- Look at the results. Do the textures remind you of the characteristics of certain fabrics? Make a note of the different effects the textures had.

Exercise 3 **Fabrics**

A broad range of media, fabrics, some trend images, and your sketchbook are required for this exercise.

– Using either trend images, actual fabric swatches, or both, experiment in a sketchbook with a variety of different media to capture the characteristics of the different fabrics.

– Think about using a mixture of natural wool fabrics, fake fur, animal print, sheer and shiny fabrics, knitted fabrics, or denim. There are so many different fabrics to choose from.
– Experiment with media and scale, drawing bigger and smaller.

Dry brushtrokes
Dip a brush into paint and remove the excess so as to get more dry strokes with the brush to get a fur effect.

Crayon/marker pen
Try a detailed approach to rendering Tartan, noticing how the colors overlap each other.

Pencil/pencil crayon
Zoom in on a knitted fabric and enlarge the knit when drawing to really understand the structure, then when confident this can be drawn in a more spontaneous way.

Pencil crayon/watercolor wash
Here you can see the development of a houndstooth style pattern.

Charcoal/wax crayon have been used here for the beginnings of this leopard inspired fabric.

Graphite stick
The tonal qualities were concentrated here to give the effects of the folds of a satin fabric.

Fine line pen/wax crayon
Here a fine line pen has been use to get the rose detail of htis print fabric with the wax crayon added last.

Pencil
Net and lace fabrics can be created with a lightness of touch, concentrating on small areas of the net and lace pattern.

Water pastel crayon and white pencil crayon have been used to give a draped shiny look to this illustration on construction paper, which also has a similar feel to the fabric seen below.

For this Dog Couture Collage, I used scraps of textures and magazine cuttings left over from other work—a lesson in being resourceful!

Assess Your Work

With a good understanding of working with fabrics, textures, and patterns, your illustrations will have a more convincing feel. On completion of the exercises in this chapter you will have learned how to:

– Use different techniques and media to create different textures or patterns
– Experiment with mark making using a variety of tools or objects
– Think about how textures and fabrics can change or enhance a silhouette

Think about the following questions in relation to your own work. Did the collage exercises make you think about your own work, or fashion illustration in general, in a different way?

– Which techniques or mark making practices have been the most successful?
– Which media do you find the easiest to use when thinking about texture?
– How will you continue to use fabric texture and patterns to develop your own personal style?

Now that you have completed the exercises in the previous chapters, you have a few basic drawing techniques that you can use to draw real garments, as well as clothes from fashion images. An inspiring place to do this might be your local costume and fashion museum, or you could draw your own clothes on a hanger or a mannequin.

Fashion illustrators often need to communicate design ideas with a high level of detail, so it's good to practice sketching key design detail features, such as folds, drapes, pleats, darts, necklines, collars, revers, shoulders, sleeves, and various fastenings. It's useful to familiarize yourself with certain types of technical language too, the names of different types of collar, for example.

Drawing Design Detail

Preperation

Make Your Own Museum Booklet

- Take an 11 x 17 (A3) piece of paper and, holding it in portrait orientation, fold it in half lengthwise (fig. 1).
- Fold the outside edges back to the fold line (fig. 2).
- Fold in half widthwise (figs. 3 and 4).
- Open out and cut or tear through the fold line (fig. 5 and 6).
- Take the outside corners and fold outward to meet each other (figs. 7 and 8).
- Fold the pages in to form a booklet (fig. 9).

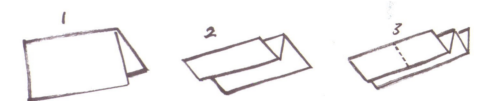

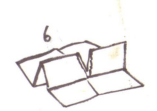

Exercise 1	**Ways of Approaching Drawing Design Detail**	Visit a museum or fashion exhibition. Take the museum booklet you have made or a sketchbook and a 2b pencil (usually at museums you are only allowed to draw with pencils). Have a look around the exhibition until you eventually find a garment you are attracted to that has elements of interesting detailing. This detail shot of a Victor and Rolf garment is a great example for drawing design details—the dart, piped edge, collar, sleeve length, pleats, fastening, pocket—there are so many fantastic details!	Try drawing in some of the ways we've covered in previous chapters: – Draw the silhouette first. – Add light and shade. – Draw the detail in.
Exercise 2	**Adding Detail First**	Use the same garment you used for Exercise 1. – Draw the detail first; for example, draw the frills on a dress or the buttons on a jacket first. – Next draw the silhouette. – Now add in the tonal qualities. – Consider how your drawing compares to Exercise 1. Which approach gave you the most interesting result?	

Exercise 3   **Developing Precision**   Choose any outfit with a lot of detail (perhaps a beaded neckline) and take the time to study and draw exactly what you see, being as precise as possible.

These are pages from an old booklet I made while sketching at the Victoria and Albert Museum in London.

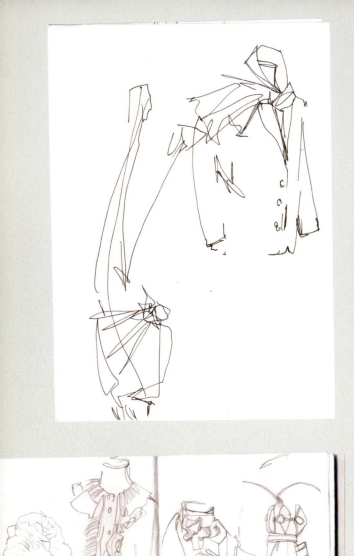

Assess Your Work

Drawing design details requires practice; when working professionally, it is essential that you portray design details, such as buttons or cuffs, with accuracy.

Upon completion of the exercises in this chapter you will have learned how to:

- Put the techniques learned in previous chapters into practice
- Focus on design details and make these the focal point of your illustrations
- Work on location: be prepared with a sketchbook or museum booklet and a range of media at all times. You may see someone or something really interesting unexpectedly, so be prepared to draw!

Further your understanding of drawing design details by asking yourself the following questions:

- Were you able to put the mark making skills you learned in the previous chapter into practice when drawing design details?
- Are there any design details that you find particularly difficult to draw? If so, what aspects are you having trouble with and why?

Exaggeration can have a dramatic impact on your work. Just as clothing itself—from corsets to shoulder pads—can be designed to exaggerate different areas of the body, illustration can exaggerate aspects of clothing or the model wearing them to create powerful images. It's up to you to decide how you use exaggeration to make a fashion statement.

Exaggeration

Exercise 1

Experimenting with Size

For this exercise you will need an 11 x 17 (A3) or 17 x 22 (A2) piece of paper, depending how your confidence has grown. You will also need an assortment of media and magazine images.

– Draw a head much smaller than you normally would, perhaps the size of a small coin.
– Draw the feet at least five times bigger than the head where you think they should be on your page.
– Draw in the hands at a size midway between that of the head and the feet.

- Create a collage for the torso and clothing areas using any materials you wish. (You could use old magazines or tissue paper, for example.)
- Paint in the legs
- Finally, add in all the details.

Upon completion, notice how the figure is more exaggerated than usual.

Here is a quick exaggerated sketch (this only took a few minutes) of a seated figure. It is very rough but has certain qualities that a more labored sketch may lack.

Exercise 2

Street Scene

- Gather a few images of figures in a variety of positions, perhaps standing in more natural poses, doing things like holding cellphones, for example.
- Draw these figures in an exaggerated way, as you did in the previous exercise. Try to vary head, hand, and foot size to play around with interesting proportions.

- Use a mixture of media to build the figures: think about line, silhouette, and tonal qualities, and bring everything together that we have covered so far.
- Try putting together a composition of exaggerated figures to see how they work together, creating a dynamic "street scene."

Assess Your Work

Exaggeration is something you will come across in all aspects of fashion design and illustration. It is therefore important to experiment and understand the power in presenting your work with exaggerated elements so that you can use this useful tool effectively.

From the exercises in this chapter you have learned how to:

- Use the techniques you have mastered in the previous chapters to experiment with exaggeration
- Understand how to use exaggeration to emphasize particular design details to great effect
- Work with more than one illustrated figure on a page. Illustrating groups of people or grouping illustrations together is a great way to present a fashion collection or equally to create powerful and striking images.

Critique your own work to increase your understanding of how exaggeration can be used to great effect:

- Is the illustration you created in the first exercise a more dynamic figure than one with less exaggerated proportions?
- How does exaggeration add to the depiction of the clothes or particular design details?

The basic techniques you've picked up in previous chapters can be used to good effect when drawing from life: for example, you could begin your work by focusing on qualities of fabrics or drawing design details. Don't be too concerned about rendering a "realistic" drawing; experimentation can give you exciting results. Changing where you begin your illustration on the paper or changing which area of the model/garment you start with can be a good way to refine your approach.

Drawing from Life

Varying Approaches to Life Drawing

I started this 17 x 22 (A2) size quick sketch, first blocking in the trousers, skirt, and blouse with a wash of watercolor. Then I added the line and detail of the model's head and other clothing in pencil crayon.

Here are the results when using different starting points, taking slightly longer for a more considered illustration. The illustrations on this page and the leftmost drawing on the opposite page were done by students in response to the example on p. 59.

In order to get some more varied illustrations, I asked the model to change outfits and try other poses (below and opposite page).

Illustration by Sara Woodward

Illustration by Catherine Mooney

Illustration by Susan Birchall

Illustration by Sara Woodward

These illustrations, a mixture of A4 (letter) and A3 (tabloid) paper, were all completed very rapidly, again starting at different points and using a mixture of media. I rarely throw any illustrations away, as there are always certain qualities I like about them, even if the figures themselves are not so well developed!

Illustration by Sara Woodward

This series of illustrations bridges the gap between this and the next two chapters, Movement and Proportion. Proportion does need to be evident in your work, but it does not need to be followed slavishly because it can make your illustrations look tight and rigid. I have purposely left this chapter until later in the book.

These illustrations are quick sketches from a live model with proportion and movement lines, again with various starting points.

These illustrations have an understanding of movement at their core.

Exercise

Using a Live Model

For this exercise you will need some 17 x 22 (A2) drawing paper, a drawing board or easel (or lean a drawing board on the back of a chair for a makeshift easel), and a variety of media.

- Find a person willing to pose for you in a variety of outfits and poses.
- Vary the time and length of poses. Work with both quick and longer sessions.
- Mix up your media and vary the starting points each time, drawing on all the techniques you have learned so far.

Assess Your Work

Working from life can be exciting to do once you have found a willing model. From the exercises in this chapter you have learned:

- Not to be scared of using color or experimenting with media when drawing from life
- Not to worry if your illustration from life is not proportionally correct—this might make it a more interesting illustration
- To work quickly: When drawing from life, there is a temptation to work slowly in order to create an accurate picture. To work as a professional illustrator, it is essential to be able to identify the key aspects of your figure—be it the interesting angle of a model's pose or a design detail such as an interesting collar—and work quickly before the model starts a new pose or changes clothes.

In order to progress as an illustrator and perfect your skills in drawing from life, answer the following questions and think carefully about which methods work best for you:

- How do your illustrations drawn from life differ from the illustrations you did from garments in a museum or gallery for the exercises in the Drawing Design Details chapter? Which do you prefer? Which did you find easier to undertake and why?
- Which poses did you find harder and why? Are there certain angles or movements you find harder to capture? Work on these!
- Which medium did you find the easiest to work quickly with and why?

Movement

Even if you draw the most conceptual, static fashions, there will always be an element of movement to them—whether in the clothes themselves or the body beneath. Clothes work with the body, and it is having an understanding of the body's movement that will make your sketching and illustration seem alive, appear energetic, and convey a certain attitude.

These exercises focus on showing movement through gesture and using movement to add a sense of character.

Exercise 1

Gesture Drawings Use a cotton swab and some India ink for this assignment.

– On an 8.5 x 11 (A4) piece of paper, draw a squiggle with a cotton swab dipped in ink. (This can also be called the "movement line"; see the Proportion chapter.) Be as expressive as you can with the squiggle.

– Look at the squiggle and draw a simple head on it. Think about the way the line bends to see what figure it might suggest.

– Add arms and legs, keeping your figure's form quite simple.

– Now draw a series of figures in the same technique across a page of the same size, on its side in landscape format. Try to make them more dynamic and energetic as you go.

This simple technique for constructing a basic fashion illustration forms the basis of a lot of the more spontaneous drawings that I do on the spot, sometimes without reference.

Follow the steps and keep the lines quick, with an immediacy that will lend itself to the illustration. Once you have the basic idea, you can then flesh out the illustrations and add impressions of clothing.

Exercise 2

Character Drawing

It is best to produce character drawings in cafés and museums, from a vantage point where you can see people milling about or standing still looking at exhibits.

- See if you can capture a whole figure in one line.
- To capture the character, start with the squiggle/movement line.
- Draw in the head and feet, and then work to flesh out the figure, working quickly since the subjects might move.

The sketches at right were drawn at the Victoria and Albert Museum, UK, and the below images were drawn at the Museum of London, UK.

Exercise 3

Developing Character Drawing

You can improve your character drawing through practice and refinement.

– Try to develop your character drawings either by redrawing a few of your sketches or by rendering them in different media.

For instance, this image has been collaged and redrawn with a wash of color added.

Here are examples of various illustrations experimenting with the movement line using collage and paint.

Assess Your Work

Creating a sense of movement in your illustrations can be difficult to master, but as a professional illustrator, capturing this is a key aspect of your job, from drawing quick sketches of models on the catwalk to a dress that is blowing in the wind.

The exercises in this chapter have taught you how to:

– Build on your knowledge of line and silhouette from the first couple of chapters and turn expressive fluid lines into elegant illustrations
– Capture energy in your illustrations

Movement is something that you will continue to refine in your illustration work. Ask yourself the following questions and see how your style progresses:

– Do exaggerated size and proportion of design details help achieve a sense of movement?
– Try exploring different media and movement. How would you create a sense of movement using collage, for example?
– Look through some magazines and find some photographs that have a good sense of movement. What key aspects of the photographs help achieve this sense of movement? Are these things that you could emulate in your own illustrations?

An understanding of proportion is essential for all illustration and fashion design work. As you will have found in the Exaggeration chapter, playing dramatically with proportion and size can create some striking effects. However, you may also wish to draw using proportions more accurate to life, while making more subtle changes such as lengthening a fashion figure through the legs a little so as not to distort the torso. Once you have learned how to draw with proportion in mind, you can choose to draw accurately as well as tweak proportions to give your illustrations their own unique aesthetic.

We measure fashion proportions by the use of "heads," as in the size of the person's head you are drawing compared to other parts of their body. An average figure is anything from 7 ½ to 8 heads in height. An illustrated fashion figure can be anything from 8 heads up to 9 ½ heads in height and beyond. There are many slightly different variations on how to measure proportion when drawing figures, but fundamentally they are all based on this principle.

The assignments in this chapter start with the basics and move on to more complex and specialized techniques.

Proportion

Proportion Basics

Use a pencil and an 11 x 17 (A3) piece of paper for this exercise.

- Fold the paper lengthwise into eight equal sections.

The following lines are marked in green on the illustration:

- Draw eight heads on the left hand side of the paper, one in each folded section, and number them 1 through 8.
- In the top section of your paper (section 1), draw a head shape in the center. Draw a straight line from the bottom of the chin down to the bottom of your page: this is known as your "balance line."
- In section 8, draw two diamond shapes on either side of your balance line to create feet.

The following lines are marked in green on the illustration:

- Draw a line 1/3 of the way down in section 2; this will be the shoulders.
- Draw a line on the fold line between sections 2 and 3; this will be the chest.
- Draw a line on the fold between sections 3 and 4; this will be the waist.
- Draw a line about 1/3 of the way down in section 4; this will be the hips.
- Draw an upside down triangle on your balance line at the top of section 5; this will mark the groin area.
- Draw a line halfway down in section 6; this will be the knees.
- Now we will join these points together (blue line).

The following lines are marked in blue on the diagram:

- Draw a line halfway down the head; draw another line halfway between the line you have just drawn and the bottom of the head, and then draw another line between these two lines. These lines will be your eyes, nose, and mouth.
- Draw two lines on either side of the head at the bottom to form the neck.
- Draw two diagonal lines on either side of the neck lines, angled down slightly and toward the edges of your paper. These will form the shoulders.
- Draw two diagonal lines from the end points of both shoulder lines, down to line for the waist.
- Draw two circles on either side of the shoulder lines: these will be used to give shape to the arms.
- Draw two curved lines from the bottoms of the circles you have drawn pointing inward to form the chest: these lines should sit below the fold line separating sections 2 and 3.
- Draw two lines from either end of the waist line down to the hip line.
- Draw a slightly curved line from each end of the waist line down to the knee line to form the thighs, and then draw more curved lines from the knees down to the top of the feet to form the lower part of the legs. Make sure your figure has two separate legs by drawing four curved lines, with the inside lines forming the inside of the legs.
- Between fold lines 4 and 5 draw in two hand shapes; for the elbow line, make slightly diagonal lines pointing upward on either side of the waist line. The hands and elbow lines are marked in purple.
- Draw in the arms (marked in red).

These are the basics of proportion. You can adapt these rules to suit your own needs; for instance, the drawing below has larger hips.

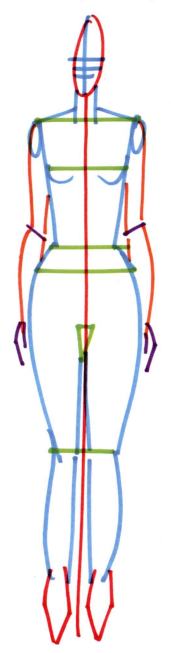

The figure at right has the shoulder, chest, waist, hips, and knee points marked with the direction they fall when the body is posed. The red central line is the balance line; imagine it as a steel rod running through the center of the body holding it up. Ensure that the feet and legs line up with it so that your figure doesn't look as if it is leaning or about to fall over. The movement line moves through the center of the figure and out over the hip. This rule doesn't need to be followed too rigidly, but understanding it will help you compose your figures.

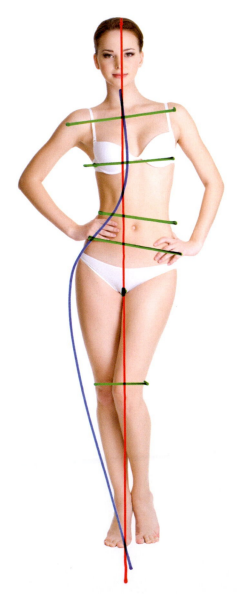

Notice how a rough croquis/template has been developed with a more natural back and neck-to-waist length. Breaking the figure into eight equal sections may seem strange at first, but once you feel comfortable with the basics you can just use it as a guideline.

These fashion illustrations based on the 8-head proportion and paper-folding technique use the lines loosely as a guide.

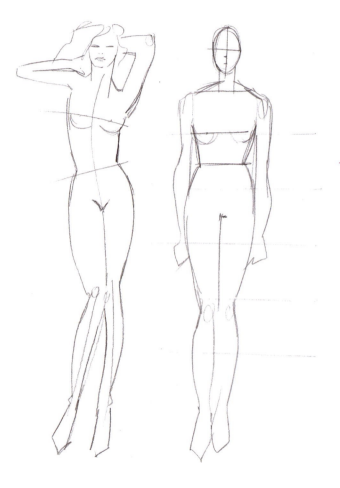

Exercise 2

Developing Your Croquis

This exercise will see you develop a series of poses suitable as basic templates or "croquis." (A croquis is a very quick drawing of a live model.) Choose poses suitable for the garments you would like to draw; for example, a pose for a figure-hugging dress may not be suitable for loose trousers.

– Draw lightly in pencil on layout paper.
– Then draw over your first drawing with various thicknesses of marker pens.
– If it helps, draw in the chest, waist, hips, and balance line.
– Vary your poses (see below).

Once you have found a simple pose you like, it can be used as a base to develop other poses. These illustrations were drawn at A3 (tabloid) size.

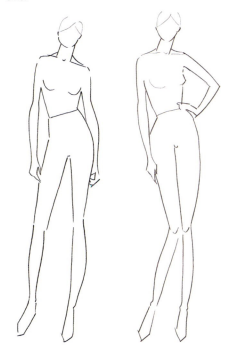

Fashion is not just about what a garment looks like from the front; don't forget the back and sides. Try to vary your poses, perhaps experiment with three-quarter views. When working from photographs, poses can be sketched with proportion and movement lines in a continuous line style. They can be kept as is or used as the basis for poses to emphasize a particular garment, for example.

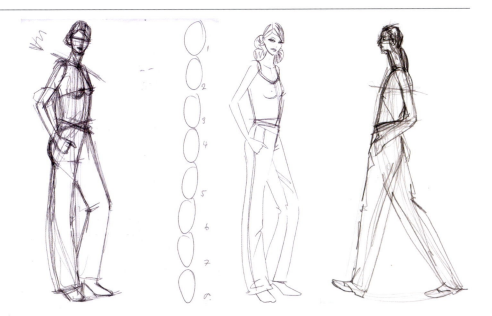

I first roughed out these trend-forecasting illustrations (below), which are based on catwalk photos, on layout paper, then refined them using a fine-line pen (above).

Exercise 3 **On Trend**

For this exercise, try finding images of various items of clothing from a fashion magazine, cutting them out, and then combining them on a new piece of paper to form an outfit, as I have done in the illustrations here, which were commissioned by a trend-forecasting agency. These were rendered in Photoshop using scanned patterns and fabric textures.

Tracing is a skill, not cheating. The illustrations below were traced, but the figure was lengthened as it was traced. It was drawn with pen and brush and ink. Note how the heavier line lifts the illustration.

Men's Templates or Croquis

Although I have only touched on drawing male figures, you can go about creating them in a very similar way to the female croquis/ templates. I have used this image to get a broken down proportionate figure and a looser sketched figure.

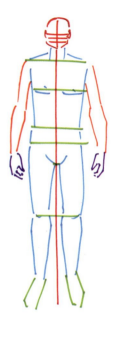

Try to vary your poses too. Here is one sketched as before.

Alternatively try a more stylized look. Sketched in a similar way to the continuous line figure in the Line chapter, this new image shows an awareness of proportion and basic figure construction.

If you frequently draw similar styles of clothing, sketch a template or croquis in pencil and use this to develop your illustrations.

Assess Your Work

The fundamental principles of proportion presented in this chapter may seem straightforward, but many people struggle to draw a figure that is in proportion. The exercises in this chapter have taught you to:

– Accurately map out and draw figures that are in proportion
– Contort or experiment with proportion to create a desired effect
– Start thinking about which poses suit which garments and how playing with proportion in an illustration can help to highlight a chosen garment or design detail

Help your understanding of proportion progress by critiquing your work and asking yourself the following questions:

– Are there any aspects of proportion that you find particularly difficult? If so, why?
– How would you adjust the proportion in an illustration to emphasize a mini skirt or a dropped-waist dress?

Faces bring your illustrations to life and add to the statement you want to make with your work. The most commonly used head positions are front view, three-quarter view, and side view.

Once you have mastered these positions, you can deviate and create your own repertoire.

You can use any medium and paper you wish for the exercises in this chapter.

Faces

Exercise 1

Front

- Draw an egg shape.
- Draw a horizontal line through the center to create two halves; this is the eye line.
- Draw another horizontal line to break the next lower section in half; this is the position of the nose line.
- Finally, draw another horizontal line halving the smallest section; this is the position of the mouth.

Exercise 2

Three-Quarter View

- Draw a slightly tilted egg shape.
- Follow the same procedure as with the front view, marking out the eye, nose, and mouth lines.
- Draw the center line a third of the way round.
- As this is a three-quarter view, you will see less of the side of the face, which is further away from you; therefore draw less of the mouth and make one eye slightly smaller.

Exercise 3

Side View

- Draw another egg shape, this time tilted diagonally.
- Follow the same procedure as in the front and three-quarter view instructions, drawing lines for the eyes, nose, and mouth.
- I will rely upon drawing the head as a silhouette to create the features of the profile.

Once you have chosen faces to illustrate, produce a rough sketch in pencil and then refine it using a suitable medium.

Drawing Faces in Different Ways

Once you have mastered most of these basics you can begin to play around and exaggerate certain features and styles and experiment with different media.

Here are a few illustrations of faces that I was commissioned to do. I used a brush pen, so when the digital image was shrunk to fit the magazine page the lines would remain clear. Above are finished illustrations, while those shown below are still at the rough stage.

This is an example of an eye. When drawing eyes, try not to make the pupil a dot, as it can make the eyes look "pinned."

Here is an example of a classic continuous-line-style face.

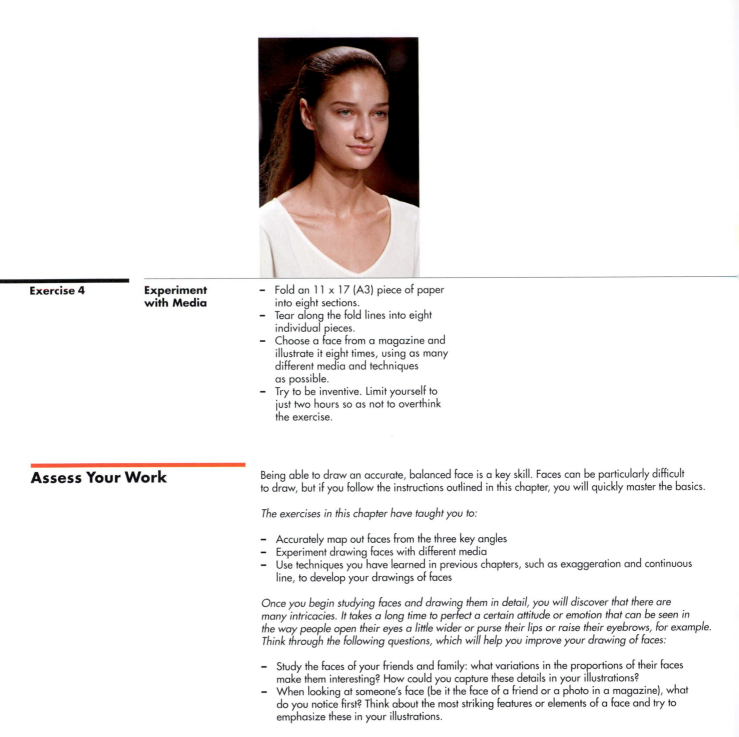

Exercise 4   **Experiment with Media**

– Fold an 11 x 17 (A3) piece of paper into eight sections.
– Tear along the fold lines into eight individual pieces.
– Choose a face from a magazine and illustrate it eight times, using as many different media and techniques as possible.
– Try to be inventive. Limit yourself to just two hours so as not to overthink the exercise.

Assess Your Work

Being able to draw an accurate, balanced face is a key skill. Faces can be particularly difficult to draw, but if you follow the instructions outlined in this chapter, you will quickly master the basics.

The exercises in this chapter have taught you to:

– Accurately map out faces from the three key angles
– Experiment drawing faces with different media
– Use techniques you have learned in previous chapters, such as exaggeration and continuous line, to develop your drawings of faces

Once you begin studying faces and drawing them in detail, you will discover that there are many intricacies. It takes a long time to perfect a certain attitude or emotion that can be seen in the way people open their eyes a little wider or purse their lips or raise their eyebrows, for example. Think through the following questions, which will help you improve your drawing of faces:

– Study the faces of your friends and family: what variations in the proportions of their faces make them interesting? How could you capture these details in your illustrations?
– When looking at someone's face (be it the face of a friend or a photo in a magazine), what do you notice first? Think about the most striking features or elements of a face and try to emphasize these in your illustrations.

This chapter involves techniques for illustrating hands and feet that combine all the other skills you have learned in the previous chapters, such as line, light, shade, and shape.

Hands & Feet

Hands

Hands are notoriously difficult to draw and can often end up looking like "bunches of bananas," as a friend of mine says. Expressive hands make a considerable difference to an illustration, so don't feel you have to hide them as most people do. As with any technique, you will improve through practice. Once you've had a go at the basic assignments in this chapter, you may wish to spend some time looking at a figure drawing book and studying the construction of fingers and joints and the way they move in more depth.

Exercise 1	**Draw Your Own Hands**	Use any type of paper and a pencil for this exercise.	– Notice all the joints, the fingers in relation to each other, the size and shape of the palm of your hand, and how your hand is attached to your wrist. Try to show all the subtle curves and intricacies.
		– Draw your own hand, the back as well as your palm.	
Exercise 2	**Using Multiple Media and Techniques**	For this exercise you'll need a variety of media (your choice) and your sketchbook.	– As you work, look at your own hands holding items like pens, cups, and scissors, noticing how the fingers grip and the shape they make.
		– On a page in your sketchbook, draw many hands in as many different media and techniques as you can.	

Exercise 3	**Exaggerating Length**	Continue using your sketchbook.

- Draw hands again, but this time exaggerate through lengthening the fingers, while keeping the palm of the hand the same size.
- Try to get all of the nuances of the line into your work.

Exercise 4	**Hands in Varying Positions**	

- Using magazine images as a guide, draw a series of hands again, in as many different media as you can.
- Draw hands in a range of positions: holding items of clothing, in pockets, on hips, and so on.
- Notice the shapes they make and exaggerate as you draw, as you did in Exercise 3.

The hands in both of these illustrations have their own kind of stylization.

Feet

It's best to practice drawing feet both in flats and in heels. Also aim to get used to drawing feet in multiple positions and from different viewpoints: front views, side views, three-quarter views.

TIP: A triangular shape not unlike a block of cheese is a good guide to start using when illustrating feet.

Drawing Feet

Use your sketchbook and a variety of media for this exercise.

- Starting with the triangle shape, spend some time doodling feet and shoes.
- Let your doodles develop by adding more media, creating some dynamic shapes—don't worry about the practicalities!

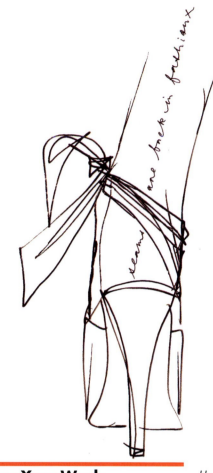

Assess Your Work

Hands and feet take a lot of practice to get right but are an integral part of every illustration, as they help finish and give expression to an illustration. From the exercises in this chapter you have learned how to:

- Get used to drawing hands and feet in different media
- Think about how you draw hands and feet proportionately in relation to the rest of your illustrated figure
- Begin to understand how you can draw stylized hands and feet that would work well with different types or styles of illustration

Critique your work by thinking about the following points:

- What media do you find worked best when drawing hands and feet and why?
- What is the best medium to use when you are trying to create a sense of movement, as in walking or dancing feet?
- Think about light and shade: how would you emphasize that a hand is in a tight fist or holding onto something heavy?

Flat Drawings: Communicating Designs

Flat drawings are used frequently in the fashion industry to communicate how an outfit is meant to look. In order to produce quick and clear illustrations for clients or colleagues, you need to know the basic terms to describe garments and details. Once you become fluent in this language and with drawing particular details, you will have more freedom of expression in your illustration.

In a former job, one of the tasks I was given was to sit in a room with a fashion designer and make a list of all the clothes that made up the collection, grouped together as outfits in the order that they would have appeared in the show in Paris. Sometimes the actual design was not clear, so I would have to talk to the pattern cutter to get an idea of what the garment might look like. All the garments had certain names, which made it easier to remember them, but I had to be very sure what the specific details of these garments were.

This is where the Drawing Design Detail chapter would have helped me. It is important to build up a good repertoire of collars, revers, and how they sit around the neck fastenings; different types of fastenings—zippers, buttons, hook-and-eye; types of sleeves—raglan, kimono, set-in; the difference between a shoulder with and without a shoulder pad. Once you have become well versed in the basics, you'll be armed with the skills to draw anything that slightly veers away from these, and you will not be fazed.

Exercise 1

Flat Drawings

Select a favorite outfit—it could be a suit, dress, jeans, T-shirt, whatever you like. Choose a winter outfit, too, as there will be more items to draw: a coat, boots, gloves, hat, denim jacket, scarves, etc.

Look at the garments individually and really pay attention to how they are made and their finishing. What type of top-stitching is used and how wide is it? What type of collar is used? Can you name it?

Lay them out flat and try to get an idea of the shape—is it loose or fitted? What type of sleeve does it have?

Lay the clothes out like you would a style sheet in a fashion magazine.

Take a photograph from above or use a mannequin if you have one; using a coat hanger is also a good way to display your chosen outfit for this exercise. Photograph half of it, or if you prefer, find flat garments in a magazine.

For this exercise use a pencil or pen and draw quickly.

– Trace the garments loosely. Here I have used a brush pen quite quickly, using fine and thick strokes. Then add a wash of color. Be sparing and loose with the color wash.

- Draw the same outfit freehand. Draw the back views, too, even though you can't see them in the original picture.

- Trace your freehand drawing, using a thicker felt pen for the outside line and a finer felt pen for the inside lines.

- Use a gray tone to add shadowed areas.

outfit ①

be Cool

Flat Drawings in Proportion

One way to make sure your flat drawings are in proportion is to use a template.

– Fold half of a letter-sized (A4) piece of paper into four sections.
– Map out your proportion lines as you did in the proportion chapter.

– Lay another piece of paper on top and draw a mannequin template. Draw half, then fold the paper. Draw a center line and trace through the other half so you know it's symmetrical.
– Draw more garments using the template as a guide to the figure. Here I've used it as an example, sketching a few versions of a jacket, blouse, and jeans. It's good practice to use the template.

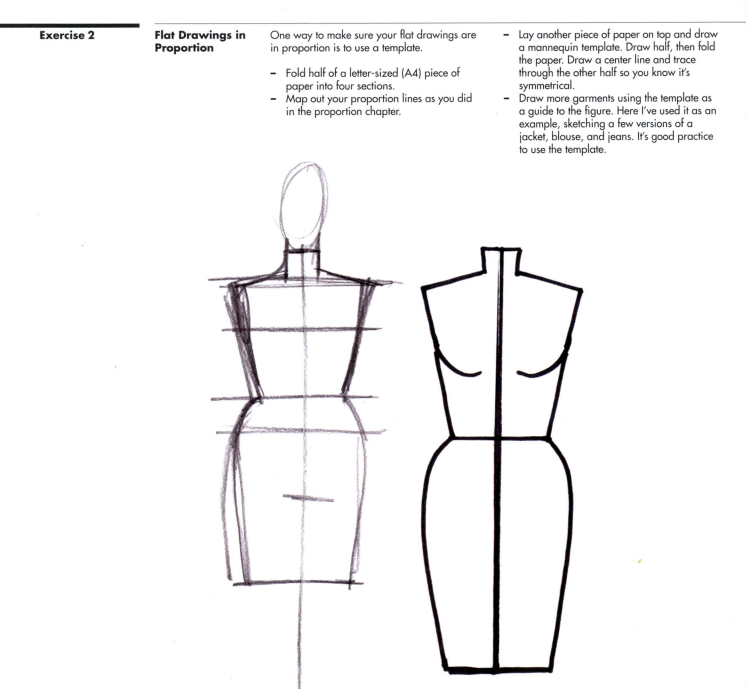

miami
LIFE

Assess Your Work

Flat drawings may seem simplistic, but they are an essential part of any professional illustrator's life. When working for a client, you will sometimes need to be able to show them exactly how a garment is made or constructed through your illustrations and how a certain look or style is put together.

From this chapter you have learned:

- The basic principles of drawing flat garments
- How to convey garment construction details in a clear manner
- How to make sure that your drawings of flat garments are in proportion

Ask yourself the following questions and keep practicing these techniques by drawing your own clothes:

- Did you feel more comfortable tracing or drawing freehand?
- Has using a template enabled you to become more confident with sketching flats freehand?
- Have you tried other media for drawing flats, adding patterns, colors, etc.?

Over the next pages, I have put together a showcase of images that cover the broader spectrum of creative fashion illustration. This is a mixture of noncommercial and commercial fashion illustration and its various uses.

Showcase

Georg Meyer-Wiel

These final illustrations for Georg's collection Papua New York make use of a variety of media and mark making. The design development page shows exhaustive research. With a great understanding of garment construction underpinning the design development stage, the style is lively and spontaneous.

Alexis Panayiotou
These beautifully evolved illustrations drawn
from a life model came out of a fashion
illustration class Alexis teaches at Central Saint
Martins. They pay particular attention to line,
silhouette, color, pattern, texture, light, and
shade and have a great understated confidence.

Audrey Ang

Notice how these brush-and-ink design research sketches by Audrey Ang for Yohji Yamamoto have a strong sense of the silhouette at their core. The dry brush strokes add texture.

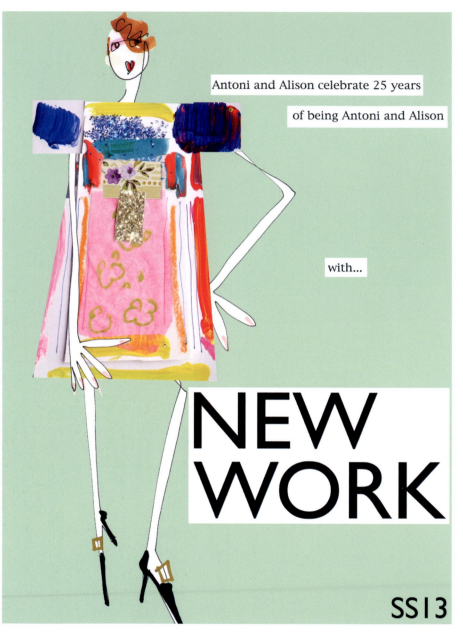

Antoni and Alison celebrate 25 years

of being Antoni and Alison

with...

NEW WORK

SS13

Antoni and Alison

Anniversary sketches from Antoni and Alison have real humor. These exaggerated sketches, collaged and computer manipulated, have personality, inviting you into the Antoni and Alison world.

She Is Wearing The Antoni & Alison 'Plain-Fancy' Dress.

Stuart McKenzie

While starting out as a fashion illustrator, I have also crossed over into mainstream illustration working for fashion magazines on editorial health and beauty commissions.

This illustration for a pharmaceutical company has great fashion attitude, and its painterly quality is manipulated in Photoshop to add texture.

Fenn Wright Manson use an illustration on an invitation previewing their latest collection.

My first commercial fashion illustration commission was for Selfridges department store. I created three illustrations that were used in store. Below are two of the original mock-ups.

In the compiling of this book, I came across images that came about through experimenting and doodling. Pages 107 and 108 contain a selection otherwise known as authorial work.

Pen and paint

The point of authorial work is to keep them and go back to them when you feel they inspire a new direction or a starting point for commissioned work.

It is very helpful to know how other illustrators work and always valuable to take inspiration from others. But the secret to being a successful fashion illustrator lies in plenty of practice and creative experimentation to develop your *own* style.

Stencil illustration

Blotted line, watercolor, collage

Collage with tissue paper

Sketchbook work

Ink blot illustration

Inspiration

It's important to get out and about and be inspired. The hardest part of starting a new illustration is sitting in front of a blank piece of paper waiting for inspiration to strike.

Museums

Museums are a great resource, and many have a costume or fashion section. Let the other collections in a museum inspire you too; look farther back into history and see what materials were being used, what stylistic choices were made, and how subject matter differed. Think about how you could use these elements in your own work.

Art galleries

Get inspired by what is going on in the contemporary art world—notice any unpredictable use of media and think about works of art you view in terms of scale, line, pattern, color, and texture. See if you can take a direct influence and let it impose itself on your work in a really obvious way. There are great opportunities in both museum and art galleries to get involved with workshops that are lead by professionals/experts/artists, and this is a good chance to speak to them of their experience in developing and mastering their craft.

Markets/clubs/concerts

Markets, clubs, and concerts are great places to people-watch; you will, without doubt, witness lots of interesting street style that you should try to sketch. Here you can see great characters already styled for you: ask if you can take pictures and use them as resources to inspire your work, or use them to try some trend illustrations. Witness the creative mix of music and fashion at gigs and clubs, and see if you can spot any emerging trends or subcultures—maybe you're part of one already! Think of the lasting influence of the swinging 60s and the punk movement of the 1970s.

Fashion magazines

Reflecting on what is current in both fashion and beauty and the arts too, magazines can act as great stimuli for starting a project. Notice how fashion spreads are styled. Try to recreate a fashion spread using your own style and choice of media. There are numerous fashion magazines to choose from. Be aware of the high-end, commercial, and more underground types of magazines too, and also where you would like to see yourself—which magazines seem to inspire you more? Don't let a magazine be the beginning and end of your research; use them in conjunction with all the other forms of inspiration.

Books

Books can set your mind free and give you the downtime you need when gathering ideas—whether it's fiction, nonfiction, poetry, biography, art books—they can inspire characters that can slip into your illustration world, and you can create narratives for them.

Toolbox

I encourage you to experiment with a variety of media, ranging in price as your pocket will allow. This way you can compare and contrast between the cheaper and more expensive media, see and feel the difference, and build up a preference for future uses.

Pencils

Pencils range from HB (hard black) to F (soft). HB are good for light mapping out and technical drawings. They produce quite a thin, hard line but are not really good for sketching. (This also applies to mechanical pencils, which are good for technical drawings and mapping out but not sketching.) Any pencils from B upward are great for sketching. Use a variety if you are working on tone, light, or shade values, and remember to use a higher number for a darker tonal area. There are also a variety of thicknesses of leaded pencils too.

Graphite Sticks

I like using a large and short graphite stick, which is great for larger sketches. Again you can determine the density of the lines made. Graphite sticks are very good for making quick expressive lines.

Roller Ball Pens

I accidentally became accustomed to using these when I was handed one and started to doodle with it. Because of the roller ball tip, there is an immediacy that lends itself to more spontaneous continuous-line drawings. These pens are available as standard writing pens and also more specialized ones for art and graphics, with tips starting from 0.5 mm—great for drawing detailed lines in specification drawings. On smooth photocopy paper, these pens glide across the surface, but with cartridge paper (heavy drawing paper), which has a slight texture, you get a much slower line because the roller ball doesn't glide across the surface so much.

Brush Pens

Using a brush pen is like having a fully loaded paintbrush at your disposal at all times. Use it as you would a paintbrush. These come in an assortment of different sized

tips. Brush pens are great for creating lines that vary in thickness and lines that trail off. Be careful not to press too hard with the tip, as it can be damaged easily and you'll get a more splintered line look. As with all pens that are ink based, remember to replace the lids because the tip will dry out if exposed to air for any length of time. The more expensive versions of these do last longer, have blending options, and usually have double-ended tips too. Frequently, I use these pens on larger beauty illustrations because the line work stands out and they are great for drawing hair, eyelashes, eyebrows, and facial features. There are brush pens, too, that are plastic and hollow with a removable head that can be filled with water, giving a similar feel to a paintbrush but with more control.

Felt-Tip Pens

As with brush and roller ball pens, the better quality pens will last longer and colors will be brighter and more vivid. Felt-tip pens also come in a variety of different tip thicknesses. More porous papers will soak up the ink and may result in more "scratchy" coverage. I tend to use these for drawing hair and face details on the smaller illustrations. Throw old, dried-out pens away—there is nothing more annoying than going through lots of felt-tips looking for ones that haven't dried out!

Marker Pens/Magic Markers

There is an art to using marker pens and suitable papers (layout paper, for example) to use them on. These pens can be refillable and come with two tips; one beveled tip and a smaller tip for detail. These are great combined with the cheaper felt-tip pens too. Magic markers can vary in the size of tip and coverage. These are great for the expressive movement line drawing and for drawing strong outlines/silhouettes. Some are permanent and some are water soluble, which means they can be used with water to create interesting effects.

Charcoal Pencils

Charcoal pencils are much easier to use than "vine charcoal" (made form burnt sticks of burnt wood), but they give slightly different results. There are a variety of different types of charcoal pencils that come in wooden and paper sheaths. Always use fixative with charcoal to fix the line work so it doesn't smudge. These work best on thicker-textured papers. Cheap, inexpensive construction papers are great to sketch on, too, and they come in a variety of different colors.

Conté Crayon

Made from compressed graphite or charcoal, conté crayons can be used in a similar way to charcoal and are great for tonal drawings.

Wax Crayons

These come in a variety of colors and are usually quite vibrant, which makes them ideal for fabric rendering. Used in conjunction with watercolors—the wax resists the watercolor—and rubbed texture, they can give expressive results.

Pastel Crayons/Oil Pastels

Pastel crayons and oil pastels come in a variety of different colors and are easily blended. These work really well on textured, colored papers and have good coverage. These can also be used in a similar way to wax crayons for certain effects.

Chalk Pastels

Chalk pastels are similar to pastel crayons and oil pastels but, unsurprisingly, are chalk based. Chalk pastels do need to be used with a fixative or finished drawings will smudge.

Colored Pencils

Colored pencils are available as soluble and non-soluble. Soluble pencils can give great effects for fabric rendering, flesh tones, and experimenting with line and wash.

Ink Pen/Dip Pen

Used with ink and a variety of different nibs, these can give a scratchy line and also a line with lots of nuance. Used with tracing paper, this type of pen can be used to create a Warhol-style "blotted" line drawing.

Watercolors

Watercolors can create dramatic effects. They take time to master, but the blending possibilities are endless, giving a transparent effect with colors blending and overlapping. Watercolors can be used on many different papers; cartridge paper and watercolor paper are thicker, more absorbent, and hold the colors well. Watercolors can be bought in block form or in tubes.

Gouache

Gouache is similar to watercolor and comes in tubes, but it is an opaque paint and is excellent for areas of dense flat color. I have used it quite thickly and also watered it down too for a more watercolor-style effect.

Oil Paints and Acrylics

Again it is good to experiment with these; oil paint takes a long time to dry and requires ventilation to work with, so I tend not to use it. Acrylic dries very quickly, so you have to work fast.

Colored Inks

These consist of dyes in a shellac solution and can be used either with dip pen or brush or whatever medium you would like to experiment with. Try experimenting with various paper types too, to see what works best for your style of illustration.

Paintbrushes

It's a good idea to get used to working with an assortment of different brush types, from the cheaper to the more expensive. The hairs on brushes can be natural (e.g., sable) or made of man-made fibers (e.g., nylon), and, again, there is a huge variety of different brush styles and tips. The more you use brushes, the faster you will develop a preference for the certain qualities that different brush styles have. Always clean your brushes immediately after using them.

Types of Paper

Experiment with a variety of different paper types, from inexpensive, white, smooth photocopy paper to white and off-white textured cartridge/heavy-duty drawing papers. If you are unsure of what's available, visit your local arts supply store. While studying fashion at college and with limited funds, I would use yellow construction paper. It's not brilliant at holding watercolors, but it was good for gouache, pastel crayons, and marker pens. Paper sizes vary and have sizes relevant to the different countries you are in. For instance, in the United Kingdom the paper sizes that I commonly use start at A4, A3, A2, and A1. Equivalents in the United States are 8 ½ x 11 or letter, 11 x 17 or tabloid, 17 x 22, and approximately 23 x 33 inches, respectively.

Glues and Adhesives

There are a multitude of different types of glues and adhesives out there. Spray mount is great for mounting presentations, while glue sticks are ideal and less messy for sketchbook, scrapbook, and collage work. Flour and water can be used too as a more economical and traditional form of adhesive.

Fixatives

Fixatives come in aerosols and are used to protect work (charcoal, pastels) from smudging. These should always be used in a well-ventilated area.

Sketchbooks

Hardback or spiral bound, the choice is yours. It's important to experiment with sketchbooks, again developing a preference for size and quality. They are objects you will want to keep; I have sketchbooks going back to my first year of art college, aged 17. Sketchbooks are great to chart the development of your style over time. Get used to carrying them around with you at all times—it's good to get used to sketching every day.

Portfolios

Keep your work safe and organized in a portfolio—you will no doubt need a size suited to the size of your work.

Index

Image Credits

Photos, pp. 10, 11, 12, 17, 22, 27, 28, 34, 39, 44, 49, 83, 86, 91: Mitchell Sams
Photo, p. 29: Somchai Som/Shutterstock
Photos, p. 41, top, l to r: Mitchell Sams, Ravi/Shutterstock, Andrew Duany/Shutterstock, Essl/Shutterstock, Africa924/Shutterstock, Natalyon/Shutterstock; bottom, l to r: JMiks/Shutterstock, Arigato/Shutterstock, Shapovalova Elena/Shutterstock, Cepera/Shutterstock

Illustrations, p. 60, left to right: Sara Woodward, Catherine Mooney, Susan Birchall, Sara Woodward
Illustration, p. 61, bottom left: Sara Woodward
Photo, p. 74: Valua Vitaly/Shutterstock
Photos, p. 80, top: stockyimages/Shutterstock; bottom 4: Viorel Sima/Shutterstock
Photos, p. 90: Denys Prykhodov/Shutterstock, Bloomua/Shutterstock, rvlsoft/Shutterstock

Photos, p. 95: Ruslan Kudrin/Shutterstock, Karkas/Shutterstock
Photos, p. 99: Adisa/Shutterstock, khuruzero/Shutterstock, prostok/Shutterstock, Tarzhanova/Shutterstock